the fat kid

Published by ECW PRESS
2120 Queen Street East, Suite 200, Toronto, Ontario, Canada M4E 1E2

NATIONAL LIBRARY OF CANADA CATALOGUING IN PUBLICATION DATA

Vermeersch, Paul
The fat kid: poems

ISBN 1-55022-515-4

1 Title.

PS8593.E74F38 2002   C811'.6   C2001-904072-5
PR9199.4.V475F38 2002

Editor: Michael Holmes, a misFit book
Cover and Text design: Tania Craan
Typesetting: Mary Bowness
Printing: AGMV MARQUIS
Author photo: Bruce MacNeil
Front cover photo: Photonica

This book is set in Garamond and Mecurius

The publication of *The Fat Kid* has been generously supported by the Canada Council, the Ontario Arts Council, and the Government of Canada through the Book Publishing Industry Development Program. Canada

DISTRIBUTION

CANADA: General Distribution Services, 325 Humber College Blvd., Toronto, ON M9W 7C3

PRINTED AND BOUND IN CANADA

ECW PRESS
ecwpress.com

the fat kid

PAUL VERMEERSCH

MISFIT

ECW PRESS

Contents

"Nobody loves a fat man."
— *Roscoe "Fatty" Arbuckle, 1907*

for Calvin Klein

An annual survey of Canada's health care system, published in May, 2001, showed that 29 per cent of boys and 23 per cent of girls were overweight in 1996, a 14 per cent increase in boys and a 9 per cent increase in girls since 1984.

— REUTERS

Author's Note

This is a work of fiction. Any resemblance between characters and events in this book and those in real life wouldn't make me feel any better.

The grass'll be greener when pigs learn to fly,
since none of the pigs'll come trampling by,
and the dirt'll be richer,
the rain'll be thicker,
and the pigs'll be happier 'n pigs in shit
gliding from barn roof to slop trough to sty.

O the world will be better
(and a shitload wetter,
if you consider the weather)
when pigs learn to fly.

Birth of a Fat Kid

Something's gone wrong in the suburbs.
     In backyards the June bugs
     are going up in flames,
and a block away it's raining, but it isn't raining here.
     Something is happening.

     Sheet lightning in the south —
across the flatland of lawns and parking lots
the tall steel cylinders and concrete poles hum
     a single note of million-watt juice
through the haywire crisscross of fat black cables
     strung over Mississauga.

It comes whirring though the green transformer
     into the yard.
You can feel it in your feet. The sign says
     Do Not Touch — It's
     dangerous.

     Relax, there's beer
in the fridge, neighbours on lawn chairs.
There's nothing much to do. It's getting dark,
     no one's going anywhere.
     Relax.

Each street, each crescent — like the city itself —
no reason to come here unless you come home to it.
     A woman

pulls her sweatshirt to her knees, calls her girls in
        from the street.

        She's pregnant again.
Can they afford this? He's coming.
He will arrive when it's cold, the air will sting
        fingers and ears, a mouth
to feed, an ass to wipe, born the morning
of the Santa Claus parade, fat and jolly, a change
of plans, and the whole day ruined
        for the girls.

●

She feels a kick and it weighs on her.
He's already shifting his weight; maybe
he's already disappointed about it.

        There will be lights.
There will be painful insults, lightning
will strike the beach, and in the morning,
a lump of glass: 6 pounds, 11 ounces.

There will be strawberry shortcake, television shows,
        tight-fitting casual slacks. . . .
There will be everything he will know in his life.
There will be everything there is to know
        about a boy.

Nativity with Pound Cake

Heavy in the crèche, the child has messed himself.
Treetop, the angel stands: store-bought, plastic, and cheap —
    but a symbol of love.
There is a genuine happiness these days, watching football,
    eating chips.
Momma says to an in-law, "Well, maybe he will be
    an astronaut someday . . . "
with a diaper pin clenched in her teeth.

All things are possible on the quantum level; think about it.
    Great antlered beasts
might race through the stars, and maybe he will be an astronaut,
    heroic and weightless someday,
but here in the world where solids have mass and shit has stink,
    this house smells like turkey
and milk gone bad, and a cigarette hangs the air
    with garlands of smoke.

This won't be the only Christmas he shits himself —
    by this time next year
he'll no doubt quadruple in weight and will actually play with his toys.
But he still won't remember the fight about the stuffing, the gravy,
    or whether the pie was burnt.
He's not part of it yet, he's outside it all, ignorant
    of worldly things
    and things beyond this world.
He is wordless and dreamless in immaculate sleep
    with Santa's head nailed to the door.

Better, Stronger, Faster
Or, The Bionic Needle

Calvin's little hand torn open on the twisted tips
        of the chain-link fence,
climbing over, up and over, already doing whatever he can to escape
gravity and the ordinary
        boredom of his world.

We can rebuild him. We have
        the capability.
He won't even need stitches — wrap the wee bugger
        in gauze and he's off —
but he will need a tetanus shot.

Compared to the quarter inch of rusty twisted steel
ripping through his palm, the slender, sterile hypo
        should be a walk in the park.
No tears in the blood for Calvin. The wound was deep,
but he proudly showed his mother, "Look . . .
        I'm bleeding."

But a tetanus shot — Jesus, a needle is different. Needles
        are on *purpose*.
Little rays of light shine from the weapon's tip, sharp
        as the needle itself.
They pierce everything in the room. They hurt.

Anticipating a whole new species of puncture wound, Calvin
screams, turns on the tears and stares the needle down

— mindless alien, bloodthirsty animal —
his instincts tell him humanity and primal fear will ward it off,
    if he only has the faith.

A doctor's office thick to the paint with one boy's wailing,
silver and white, sterilized and cold, antiseptic, polished, shirtless,
    inhuman.

Peace, child. Silence, love. Calm down. Listen.
    This is a bionic needle.
It will make you just like The Six Million Dollar Man.
You want to be like The Six Million Dollar Man,
    don't you?

●

Something changed then. The winds died away,
    the storm abated, the Lord
    walked on water, collapsed
buildings flew back together again, and Calvin
    sat up straight —
    Bring it on.

Running in circles on the lawn at dusk, Calvin,
    secure in the knowledge
he would soon be lifting cars with one hand,
the hand so carefully bandaged now.

    He would be better, stronger, faster.
When this comes off, he whispered to himself, wide-eyed,
    giddy with its influence,
when this bandage comes off, I'll show 'em. . . .

●

He quietly believed it for years — as he grew,
thin copper wires were replacing his veins.
He knew in his heart, he could tell, he could feel it —
 the needle was taking effect.

Left-handed Till He Was Five

Because he was so heavy and so high
        in the tree,
because gravity had its hold on little Calvin,
because if you stick a toothpick in a grapefruit
        and drop it,
                the toothpick'll snap.

His hand was hanging down around his elbow
        after the fall,
like a glove sewn on an empty sleeve,
                just dangling.

Climbing trees was against the rules in those days —
                gravity doesn't care
how much you hate being heavy.

They asked him how he broke it, so he told them
        he fell off the tube-slide
        in the playground, and so
they tore it down forever.

Almost immediately he began colouring with his right
        instead of his left,
and the rest of his life felt a lot like how that crayon felt
        in his hand.

Campbell's Soup

Campbell's tomato soup with crackers and
a grilled cheese sandwich, his favourite.
    Back then the kitchen
had a lot of yellow and it made the light
    seem warmer.

He had a blue turtle placemat and loved
    setting his spoon on the eyes —
a good boy all morning could watch
    TV with lunch.

It didn't matter what was on; everything made him laugh
    when he was eating.
He laughed at his spoon-eyed turtle; he laughed
    at the funny puppets; he laughed
when someone else laughed, and he laughed at his dog,

and when his mother made her mosquito face and went
    buzz buzz buzz he laughed,
but he cried when he got in trouble for saying the "F" word
    like Uncle Ronny.

He cried *Mommy, I'm not bad, I'm not, I didn't*
    mean to, and he cried
    I'm sorry in his soup.
He got a spanking when his dad got home, then went to bed crying
the drawn out *hoos*, then fell asleep,

then a dream about steam-diggers, then

a day with no TV and a visit with his old aunt Bette, whose house
    smelled like camphor and salami,
and whose wrinkles were scary when she got too close, and who spoke
    with an accent he didn't like.

She fed him everything he wanted, more soup, another sandwich,
    gave him candy,
and told him not to go into the room down the hall
    where his dead cousin used to sleep, and where
a picture of Donny Osmond grew dusty on the shelf.

She fed him everything he wanted, more soup, another sandwich —
it made him happy, made him full, made him sleepy — it made him
    everything he is today.

Come See What's on Sale Now at Sears

Attempting to squeeze his fat little legs into eight
       different pairs of pants —
corduroy, blue jeans, dress slacks, sweats — without
       once taking off his shoes,
as pair after pair keep draping themselves
over the change-room door, greeted
       from the other side
by his mother's voice saying, "Here, try these on,
       and these, and these. . . ."

The room is four by four by twelve, and the boy
       is five foot three.
It's even versus odd, and everything seems twice as big
       as everything is
in the sweat-speckled mirror.

The dusty 60-watt bulb, the gum-covered rug, the smell
       of stale air — what is it?
The scab of flesh-tone paint flaking off
       the end of the mannequin's nose?
There's something *not right* about this place — he can feel it
       in his skin.
He exhales all the air from his lungs, sucks in his gut and holds it.
       He's getting bigger.

And he can hear the saleslady talking to his mother,
       "No, these don't come in a larger size."
And a frustrated woman pleads with her son,

"Honey, let *us* have a look."
They want to help him. They are dying
        to lift his shirt,
pull at his waistband and click their tongues
        because the clothes don't fit.

Why won't they leave him alone? The boy can't breathe
and the buttons are gathering steam, preparing for flight,
        and all the zippers
on all these pants are pulling and stretching themselves
like desperate little mouths that have been sewn shut
        but need to scream.

A Fat Kid Watches a Snake
Eat a Toad at Camp Ololondo

"I am too big, too big by far. Pity me."
— Elizabeth Bishop, from *Giant Toad*

Our Lady of Low-fat Dog Food,
everything here is opposite of good.
The fat kid is fat; the toad is half-
      alive; the mess
hall's starting to reek of the ruddy beginnings
      of meatloaf, and who knows,
maybe the beginnings of life — some staffer tryst
      in the mop closet, or
some egg about to hatch in the crumbs,
      whatever. The fat kid
watches a snake eat a toad ass-first, the topaz eyes
      swell to rubies
      with one more slack-jawed gulp.

Finally the toad spreads its gums, gives up the ghoul
      and a critically injured cricket, too,
skidding away from all this, silently, on one hind leg.

Aromas and gathering-noise waft in from the mess hall, the bell
      will sound any second.
There isn't much time, he'd hoped there would be, there should be . . .
      the fat kid
      looks for a stick.

Calvin Was Curly

Whenever they pretended they were
    the Three Stooges
at recess — eye-poking, knucklehead
    rehearsals, routines —
Brian was their brave and idiot Moe,
and Nelson was sometimes Larry (though
    sometimes he was Shemp,
it really depended on his hair),
    but Calvin was always Curly.

He danced the Curly Shuffle, mastered floor spins,
    got the laugh down pat.
He was Curly in math class, and on the playground
    in effeminate yellow track suits
he was Curly — in October Calvin wore banana-cream
    from the boys' department at Sears —

Chiffon balloon lovely, one
could almost see the string set free
and believing he might float away
    try to catch him. . . .

And he was Curly, still Curly, as moustachioed
eighth graders ground sand in his hair, Curly
    as they muddied
his brand new track suit with ball-diamond dirt
and poked his curly ribs with a Louisville Slugger,
    asking if it tickled.

Calvin was Curly walking home at four,
        brushing off the dust and mud,
Curly moving past his sister watching soaps
        in the kitchen —
but wait, he almost wasn't Curly for a moment,
his reflection in the window there,
        against the early dark,
a glimpse of his red and puffy wet-cheeked face,
        the Curliness
fading in and fading out of him. . . .

●

But he *was* Curly, of course, he was Curly on the edge
        of his curly little bed,
Curly as his curled fist came to his nose again and again,
        and made the Curly blood,
ten years in the flowing, flood his dirty banana-cream clothes.

Curly the head round which the whistling birds encircle,
Curly the ring of stars, the pulp of cartilage, Curly.

His pillowcase accepted this new colour now —
        once cornflower blue and white
adulterated by impressive red dots, blood stars, pricks,
        and the comet tail spreads
from wiping his face. He was Curly, and the splatters
that come from sputtering sobs are actually quite intricate,
like veins of red ore on his hands and sleeves,
        and Calvin Little,

the fattest kid in school, as he wept and bled and hated it,
    with all his love of comedy,

    was Curly.

Derek Mitchell

All the boys were ten but none of them
could have been more ten than Derek Mitchell,
a real good-looking, athletic little kid —
it wasn't just his mother who thought so.

In twenty years no less than ten
maybe fifteen women turning thirty
will tell their friends about the first boy
they ever did anything with,

and they'll be talking about Derek Mitchell.
Mitch, they called him. Go Mitch!
Fifth grade home run champion. Fast, elastic,
tanned like he stored solar power in his skin.

God damn Derek Mitchell with his leonine hair
and harem of flat-chested crush-girls, the hero
and the envy of the boys — he had
a genuine pair of his dad's old baseball pants

and he wore them to school like an MVP. His nunchuks
were fashioned from two lengths of broomstick —
he knew how to use 'em, too, show-off with
Bruce Lee moves at recess — the centre of attention

till Mrs. Sprawl took the god damn things away,
but not before Mitch (nice goin') split his own face
at the eyebrow. The first kid in class to need stitches,

or crutches, or a brace for his knee. A Warrior. Mitch

picked his fights and won most of 'em, wasn't
afraid to bleed on his new clothes because
he wore his brother's old ones. He was ten and on top,
at his peak, in his prime — and he walked that yard
      like he knew it.

Kryptonite Safety Pin

"What doesn't kill you . . . really, really, really, really hurts."

— Ronan Quinn

A clasped barb fastens a red towel
around a boy's neck and lets him
be who he'd rather be — truth, justice. . . .
       The heart is an organ

pumping blood to the chubby extremities,
hands clenched into fists, the legs sometimes
moving faster than they ought, and he's so
       glad of it, glad of his legs.
Please let him have these nine or ten seconds —
       the girls are watching.

They lie on their bellies and elbows, they lie
       on picnic tables beneath
       a big brown pagoda in the park.
They cheer him on. They lie. They titter when
the towel gets snared on a nail and the clasp
       snaps open. . . .

SNIKT!   SHLLLLLT!   ARRGGHH!

The steel barb carves a shallow groove across
the fat boy's throat. They titter the heartwarming
       laughter of girls (so often
heard from the kitchen window as kitten-shaped
       cookies are baking for the

last day of school), they titter
        as he stumbles, scrambling home, his hands
wringing his own neck from the sting. They lie
        on their bellies and elbows,
tittering, joyful, best friends forever — they paint this
        on the table in glittering nail polish.

●

Later on, his neck will heal. Later on, the girls will turn
        on one of their own. The one
        they least like, the least pretty —
they will accuse her of wanting to marry him.

Obsession For Men

"Between love and insanity lies obsession."
— Calvin Klein

At the church picnic Calvin learns
      a new expression
from the old birds in the choir.
"Like a workhorse in a wool suit,"
      they say,
as in, "Good Lord, that fat kid sweats. . . ."

Well, it's not his fault the picnics are always
      in summer,
and who wants to play stupid baseball anyway?
      All you do is run.
Calvin would rather sit and read the magazines
      his sisters left in the car.

He sits alone on a patch of grass, his paper plate
piled high with fried chicken and french fries,
      flipping past
the women in makeup, the men in behind them,
when all of a sudden a ribbon of girls runs by,
      chasing after a frisbee
as though the frisbee itself were rich and famous
      for being chased
      by ribbons of girls.

The pages of *Vogue* fall open to an ad
      for Obsession —

underneath the dangerous chestnut tree, the burning
      picnic sun,
Calvin tears into the sample and rubs it
      on his wrists and neck.

The wet paper leaves trails of white chemicals
through the perspiration on his skin, and the man in the ad
stares out at Calvin in war paint, saying,
      "Congratulations,
you are like me now. You are like me."

●

The man is slender and boyish with high cheekbones,
wearing a gorgeous linen suit with no shirt
      in the back of a limo, in
downtown Milan. He is
on his way in style to eat midnight
      delicacies with the beautiful
daughter of a wealthy Belgian chocolatier, no doubt,
in a lavish silk and marble apartment that
      overlooks the lights. He is

a man who knows seduction is not a game, is not
      a democracy. He is
looking fabulous, smelling fantastic,
      and this is his world. His. He is

sweating like a workhorse in a wool suit. He is
      brushing away the ants
that try to eat the gravy on his leg, while

he pulls at his scrotum
as it sticks to his thigh in the heat.

His plate piled high with fried chicken and french fries,
        sitting by himself below
the dangerous chestnut tree, the burning picnic sun.
        He is
looking at pictures of women in Wonderbras, and men
so thin they might be made of paper so glossy
        they even shine at night,
while the parishioners search feverishly for that other jar
        of olives.

●

Our boy is gentle, young and bright,
and this is his world. His. He is
looking fabulous, smelling fantastic.

Wonder

John Forestall's father has about six thousand
      dirty magazines hidden
in a suitcase under the stairs — the boys figure
Mr. Forestall must sneak down there all the time
      to peek at them
while John's mom is sleeping, to smoke
      his smelly old corncob
and drool over Cindi's bare boobs, Maggie's bum.

John thinks Miss November's the prettiest, and Rob
really likes Nurse Edna, but no one else does.
      She's ugly.

Not one *Hustler* in Calvin's house — he looked.
      And being too young to buy one,
Calvin uses pencil crayons, tries to draw Wonder Woman
      without the golden eagle protecting
her breasts, with the star-spangled underwear
      pulled away, still clenching
the magic lasso at her hip, still a princess trimmed
      in tiara, bullet proof
bracelets and high-heeled knee-high boots.

He likes to draw. It's something he can do
      with the TV on. It relaxes him
colouring navy blue highlights in her hair and giving her
      big big big red lips.

But he doesn't know what to draw, really —
            fish-eye nipples
on improbable tits, a waistline like Betty Boop's,
            and of course the impenetrable shield
of tight black curls to hide what he can't yet fathom,
the smooth riddle of undressed dolls, and he's sad
            because he doesn't know
why each time he tries this her eyes look so angry.

A Four-eyed Pig

As if being a pig wasn't bad enough, now Calvin needed glasses.
A pig with glasses — that's perfect — a four-eyed pig.

Doctor Watson the optometrist puts Calvin at ease with idle chatter.

"Did I tell you my sister passed away? Her kidneys you
know. Here put these on, these are the same frames my dad
wears. He never complains about them, in fact he loves
them, he told me himself. He says before he got these glass-
es things were a lot worse than they are now, if you can
imagine things being any worse Calvin, because I can't.
Things are bad enough as they are. Did I mention my sis-
ter passed away? Well she did."

The glasses only made Calvin's head hurt for a few days, which
isn't so bad when you think about it — most pigs get slaughtered and
turned into bacon.

Predestination

"He will not say that chance has made him different from the brutes. . . ."

— John Calvin

Even if you're born damned, you still have to work your ass off
       to look good.

"Out of all your father's sperm I can't believe *you* were the fastest,"
       says a lean, mean kid
to Calvin, last in the lap around the playground again, and no one
       the least bit surprised.

Well, maybe Calvin would've been another Calvin — same kid only
       with a more pronounced chin, trim
and slender, graceful, faster, a few inches taller, better clothes, better
       hair, but not this, not this thing —

if only a more ferocious cell had won the egg race. . . .

Maybe he'd even like salad and be popular. It's not so hard
       to believe, and what would he lose?
That blond hair? Those green eyes? Big deal! His love
       for that silly old
                         trombone he can't even play?

(He used to sit with it for hours in the backyard, buzzing his lips,
       no talent for music, until
the neighbours complained, and his sisters told him: *it's over, Calvin,
       it's over.*)

Brave in the race again, once more around: tree stump, flagpole,
    swing set, home. . . .
Don't think he'll quit on account of the sword that effort has driven
    through his ribs (don't think that
for a second). What, and face the obvious?

Don't slouch. Sit up straight. Clean your face.
We'll get you a better haircut next time, we promise.

Calvin Little and the City of Boys

Here in the swamp the boys have dragged
lumber stolen from construction sites
to build a city in the trees. In their minds
this is civilization. Rungs nailed up the trunks.

Calvin sits astride the burly biceps of an oak,
saying *na na na* to gravity's bloody contract,
saying I am a monkey, I am lighter than leaves,
then leaf-light he leaps to land a branch away.

Sure-footed on the next limb, he fists the nails
in his pocket, all sizes. They stab at his palm,
feel like ancient weapons, the evolution of claws.
Up goes another rung on the great ladder up.

There isn't a father for miles around who knows
where his hammer is. The blackened thumbnails
go unexplained. So-and-so twisted his ankle
falling off his bike. Do not speak of the City of Boys.

Summer is only four months long. Next year
the boys will come here only half as much.
New subdivisions will uncurl their asphalt fronds,
and all these acres will be turned to basements.

Next year the boys will turn thief again, retreat
deeper into the swamp, all the animals will follow
as the bungalows rise up. At night the boys will piss
on fresh drywall and drag floorboards away in the dark.

The fat kid, the tall boy, the short guy, the brain —
high above the mud. This place was made for them.
It is Saturday and Calvin nails on another rung,
the same boy he was last year — only taller,
        and wearing different shoes.

Cannonball

Poolside, the girls were a bag of fruit candy
    in their swimsuits,
      watermelon pink and green,
and Courtney's tangerine two-piece hinting
at what next summer held for her body.

The boys all started taking off their shirts,
a montage of navels, muscles and spines,
but Calvin kept to his faded blue T and tried
    to look thin trying to look
like he wasn't looking at the girls.

He yelled CANNONBALL and jumped while
    everyone swam to the sides —
the backsplash got the windows wet,
    and the parents in their chairs.
His classmates cheered, and called him Moby Dick —
    they begged him to do it again.

The Purple Nurple

There is nothing else in nature so effective,
        a tornado of seizures
bound in a knuckle. It's easy:

        simply pinch the nipple
between the thumb and pointy finger
        and wrench it around
four hundred degrees or so.

Yes, child, the flesh *is* weak. See,
        the resulting bruise
takes the shape of mini-sunbursts.

The nipple is where the nerves have built
        little balconies into the world
from which to expose themselves.

Ask a nipple if it knows the feel of gravel
        embedded in the skin.
Now ask your knees.

        Primate behaviour has
unaccounted-for variations.
        For instance: young male
        chimpanzees will
wrestle and fight and punch and
bite to establish dominance,

much in the way of adolescent boys,
        but for some reason
our cousins the apes have not included
the purple nurple in their rituals —

perhaps they're not evolved enough.

Ask Calvin Little, age 13,
        breathless on his knees
in the gravel, crying uncle,
if he doesn't believe it takes a certain
amount of logic and reasoning
        to conceive of torture.

Golden

Separated from the pack again (when
       wasn't he?), hands tacky
with honey dipping sauce, vanilla shake dribble
       dripping down his chin,
sitting all proud and round and high
       on the short wall surrounding
       the patio.

Large this, large that, make it a double,
fifty billion came before this, that's just
       the beginning.
       Fifty billion, each one
identical — a thousand chefs and scientists spent
       their lives perfecting it.

The heat from the sun, from the parking lot, squeezing
       the juice from his skin —
holding the cup's cold to his face, he fans his shirt — inside
       his pale, rubbery torso shimmers
with noon moisture, clear skies, and the cars kicking up
       dust and napkins, swirling little
       eddies and devils.

They Speak of Their Little Brother

Mom . . . Dad . . . .
We can't make him beautiful, but we can try.
    We can dress him up
in a nice white suit and give him a perm,

    but it wouldn't do any good.
New shoes, new glasses that don't say geek,
    or better yet, ditch
the glasses and get contacts, wash his face

    with Clearasil — and nothing.
No improvement. Face it, the hair on his face
    looks like lint on a pill.
He has to shave, and even then he's just gonna eat

    and eat until dinner,
getting fatter on television and rented videos,
    drawing superheroes
with his school supplies, fabulous legs and chests,

    male and female. We have to
tell him to stop, we have to tell him it's important
    to look good, and tell him
not to cry. Nobody, not even a guitarist, looks good crying.

●

And he does cry,
when he's alone and it hits him — he wants it all:
    the job, the money, the car,
the girl. He wants it all and he wants it now.

    The television he loves
keeps telling him: *You're nothing if you don't*
    have it all. The actors,
the singers, the wrestlers, the winners have it all,

    and right now he believes,
more than he believes that God and greens
    are good for him,
there is a better-than-average chance he never will.

The Best a Man Can Get

I

Television promises that a man shaves bare-chested,
      wrapped at the waist
in a crisp white towel, and when he's finished,
      a beautiful woman appears
from another room (where she has been advertising tampons
      or fabric softener
or maybe razors for women). She is naked

except for the clean, pressed shirt that gathers the scent
      of her body, her perfume,
the shirt he will wear to the office that day to remind him
      how she caressed his
smooth face and chest with manicured nails, and made
      that silent *Oh* with her mouth.

      And America understands —
when the commercial is over, they will take each other's hands,
      and being perfectly clean they will go
      giddily into their sunlit boudoir
      before they go to work.

II

Unfortunately for Calvin the towel is blue
     with red and yellow
sailboats, and his shirt isn't clean or pressed,

but he shaves everyday for the hell of it, for the steam
     and the cream and the steel of it,
     despite the possibility of blood,
     because he knows, he's been told,
     the more often he shaves the darker
     and thicker his beard will be,
so that one day it will make a better mask.

Occasion to Be Photographed

They are beautiful on purpose tonight.
They have been getting dressed
        for this dance
all their lives. All their lives
they have been doing their hair
        in preparation.

        This dance
is the dance that will make or break
their recollections of being green and easy,
        and whether or not
living through it was worth it.

        Whether or not
it was worth it to weather the years
before they had to think twice
about whether or not it was worth it.

        This night
is the night most prominent
on the rocky cliff of being cared for,
        a promontory
into a sea of self-reliance, of earnings,
        of lost virginities.

        One of those occasions
of such magnitude — as in being married,
        or arrested, or found

mangled in some cheap motel — it is necessary
    to be photographed.

Those who can promenade will promenade,
    and those who cannot
will drink punch and try to look as happy as possible
    for the light-of-foot,
or they will try to be drunk, or
    they may stay at home
downplaying the importance of it all.

Sick (A Sermon)

He was sick
deep down to his pork-bellied future,
deep inside the insulated miles
    of intestines wrenched
by doubtful quantities of wedding cake,
    by beautiful bare knees
bound to rest aside much slimmer hips,
    certainly guts wrenched
by the morbid buffoonery of every
    acceptable fat man on TV,
    he was sick.

He was sick
of the kisses and invitations flying
    like rich kites above
the low-lying slums of the ugly,
the dizzying heights reserved for those
    who walk on air
above the low-lying slums of the ugly.

He was sick
right down to his great big bones, I tell you,
right down to his big fat bones,
    sick to the teeth
of the whole wholesome big-boy load
of homework handed in on time
and the teacher's doe-eyed faith that
    the fat kid don't

cause no trouble, the fat kid's a good boy,
a shy boy, the fat kid don't cry.

Who's gonna mine their way through his life
        to hold those bones,
        to cling to those bones,
who's got the will to see through walls,
behold the perfect slimness of those bones?

        He was sick
after mealtimes, the belly ache, the body
rejecting the transplanted cow flesh, potato flesh,
        and the sweetly suicidal
death-by-chocolate reminder of his sickness . . .
        à la mode.

Alla Kazam! Alla peanut butter sandwiches!
        He was sick

        — sick of wrestling light
in the shadow of popular sisters, sick
        of all the reflections, all the
        pressures and reputations,
losin' his lunch for all the sticks and stones,
        and their verbal proxies,
that is to say nauseous of the nomenclature of fatness
        and his parents' friends
calling him *Big Guy* or *Bubba,* or *Beanpole* or *Slim*
        if they were feeling *ironical.*

Oh for heaven's sake, he'd take the stick and stones —
if the sticks and stones would promise to keep their mouths shut.

Seasick, airsick, carsick,
unwell of the wardrobe of fatness, the poses and postures
of fatness, he was not
a hundred percent of those men in the underwear ads . . .
and sick (when the sickness
had the strength to work its way through the grotesque
thick wads of his body)
from head to toe, sick
of the question: how many fat kids does it take
to screw in a light bulb?*

So sick he swore by the god that made him — *I will not eat
your cooking anymore!*
It tastes like a fat man's life; it tastes like eating alone.

All errors and no eros make Cal a dull boy —
what's it gonna be, kiddo, the cheese or the knife?

*One. The rest clear out the fridge.

Teenage Phoenix

This is the ceremony of another age.
       Bring out your dead.
A pack of juvenile humans have established themselves
       in the field behind the house.
The males who have their choice of willing females
       are dominant. The rest
learn the values of compromise and steadfast allegiances.
       They drink themselves content.
       Bring out your dead.

Gone are the pillowcases and plastic pumpkins filled
       with fistfuls of nosebleed caramels.
Gone the fairy princess. Gone the cowboy. Gone the ghost.
       False faces now are subtle in the guise
of loose connections, mild friendships. God isn't telling
       Adam that he saw Eve giving Satan a blowjob.

       Many fires have been lit.
       Bring out your dead.

The fat one among them is Calvin. He's been hiding
his erection for the better part of an hour. Looking
for phantom keys or change in his khaki pockets.
       Bring out your dead.
       Not only the pea-sized
silhouettes, but also the colour of Courtney Miller's nipples,
       are plain as day in her skin-tight whites.
Nothing to do but have another beer and

bring out your dead.

Out back of the fence in a heap of leaves
Calvin steams a jet of white-hot piss, none-too-sure
      where the cigarette came from,
      none-too-sure he even smokes.
      The spinning zip-up as he wipes
a droplet of urine from his hand to his shirt —
before he trips into that push-up position, palms down
in the embers of that afternoon's leaf burning.
      Bring out your dead.

In the sixteen years that seemed a simple
lightning flash from his birth, an X-ray snapped
against the leaden apron of Halloween's dusk,
      his bones were unmistakable.
In the short seconds it took his brain to register
      his flesh was burning,
      it registered —
this wasn't going to impress any of the girls.
      Bring out your dead.

      The blisters were the size of bottle caps.
      Behold the son!

Lead him to the bird bath where his wounded hands may soak.
Bring him a bottle of Dave's dad's scotch,
      that he may feel no pain.
Light another cigarette for him; let the ashes fall in his crotch.
Help him, help him come up with a good explanation for this.
      He is your friend. He is not your friend.

He is the wounded, the butt, the scapegoat, the lamb.
    Behold the son!

●

He will eat breakfast with blistered hands and tell the tale —
    how he saved that young girl's face
    from the flaming marshmallow
    that flew from God-knows-where.

He will eavesdrop on the phone and learn the news —
Alex Matthews, Kristine Hack, and Jeremy Whatshisface,
    kids he barely hated —
the quintuple roll and the fireball on Waterworks Road.
    Bring out your dead.

Alone in the Bathroom He Removed His Shirt

God how he admired the scarecrow and Jesus
on the cross, sunken gut and ribs you can count.
Alone in the bathroom he removed his shirt,

neatly folding it over the back of the toilet
he examined himself, sucked it in — he only stood
on the scales when he was naked and dry.

His belly ached empty. One monastic bowl
of porridge every three days, that was it.
For lunch he'd bike 60 kilometres,

then drink a glass of water. You need to have water.
He stayed home from school, lied about nausea,
lounged by the pool in Bermuda shorts getting a tan,

somehow thinking the sun would shrink him faster —
as near as possible to vanishing, but not quite.
In time the pangs inside became a tingle,

like after coming. He grew thin and cried for joy
the day he punched a new hole in his belt.
He turned in front of the mirror half the day

becoming a small white flower, becoming almost
seventeen years old, as the ribs began to emerge
like cypress roots in a barren season. He craved

to count them all and find one missing.

A Girl's Disease

Though he was still dying, he kept it shush and they praised him —
        their own little daisy stem.
When Kathy Skin-and-Bones finally packed it in and they buried her
        long and narrow in a rifle box,
        they finally knew:
she wiped steam off the mirror and looked into a funhouse world
        with a thousand fat ladies
        all wearing her bathrobe.
They're the ones that killed her — gave her the girl's disease.

One third of him gone to follow her, they praised the rest and took it
        to the tailor, the whole
chalk-and-needle treatment, the works. He finally had an ass
        that didn't make his pants look fat,
        an ass worth spending money on.
All this and some praise for a little daisy stem, one third gone.

And he went to the vigil on the football field; they all went,
        since they got out of class.
They lit candles in plastic cups and sat through a priest and feedback.
"Kathy was important to our school. . . ." Reverb squelched the rest,
        "to all of us," is what he said.
        The truth is that's not true.
Six maybe seven people there would miss her, but they'd get over it,
        go home to their own shit.

●

Look around, little daisy stem, who's gonna care
when you turn brittle and break at the waist?
Who's gonna believe a big boy's got the girl's disease
        when the balance tips
        and you go slipping off?

The Ultimate Weight-loss Program

Only a figment of an animal eating
    you alive, or ghostflies
nibbling your meat, and the woozy,
    dog-tired room-spins
when you reach for the railing, but you're
    showing your corpse who's boss!

Results the first week guaranteed, and it doesn't
    cost a cent. No more sweating
at rest, ruing your youth, done with the two-man slacks.

The days will pass like picking daisies once
    you get accustomed, learn
not to listen to the voice in your limbs, the lactic moans
    pleading for the end.

A Bad Dream of Wings

I

Going back now, the oops of his birth, the shock,
     it was all very plain —
there was aching, and words, and worry, but everyone survived.
No bystander cradled a trumpet; no prayers were said;
     no calls were placed to reporters.
Just a breath and a push and bingo, there he was, third in line.

But suppose when the water broke a faint screech came
     from the belly,
and halfway out the wet downy folds on his back
     began to beat against her thighs,
and in her arms the hatchling straightened out his neck
     and gaped his gob
       for a meal of rat.

Inhuman certainly, but you must understand —
it would have saved him all those years of pointless arm flapping.

II

Or maybe not. Remember that cartoon?
The clumsy dragon with the bright orange tuft of hair
    was so fat
his puny little wings could barely lift him off the ground —
he'd snort his frustration through a puff of smoke,
    then smile in embarrassment.

    Calvin had the T-shirt.
He wore it like a totem when they told him to ship out.
There's this specialized camp, you see, for the pin-stickers
and cutters, for the match-fingers and pill-takers,
    for the darling little starving ones —
    all the crazy kids who wanna die.

Camp Get-A-Life Activity Schedule

On Monday you can be Robin Hood
and foil Prince John, or Geronimo, proud.
Suction cups on glass are sharpened flints
piercing the throats of your demons.

On Tuesday, you can be the great master,
the Michelangelo of Popsicle sticks and macaroni,
but first you must *believe*.

By dinner on Wednesday you will be expected
to know the names, as well as the psychiatric profiles,
of your fellow campers. Listen well,
dessert will be at stake. And Wednesday's turtle pie.

Thursday . . . Thursday they start to prepare you,
teach you Bernoulli's principle,
teach you about wind.

Then Friday they take you up, demonstrate
a few simple turns,
the defenceless world at two thousand feet.

For a treat, on Saturday, they'll tell you
    "You have control"
    halfway into a nose-dive.
(The barn plus the highway plus the gravel pit plus acceleration.)
Don't worry. You will not have control.

When Sunday comes you will eat the best creamed corn
    you've ever had in your life.

Don't Cry, Annabelle

She was the pretty dark-haired cutter. Annabelle,
who carved a notch in herself each time the house
felt too cold. "Like counting days in prison,"
she says, "it's the only way to keep track."

He was the fat kid who wasted away. Calvin,
who starved himself marvellous because
the billboards told him to, high on their building-sides
like treasure maps or guiding stars to the adoration.

There's such a tiny rift between the divine acts of love
          and the wretched ones.
The wretched ones whispered throughout the electric maze
          of the brain, inches from the dead ends
where, cut off and missing, you sense that once again
          the house is freezing.

Annabelle and Calvin sit on steps in the flesh world,
opening up, passing between them a confessional smoke.
"But you're so beautiful," he says, defying her lacerations
and their logic, scaling the rubbery walls of his girl-fear.

Then she points out, as though her voice were pointing out
a galaxy, her words showing him that exact place in the heavens
where he would discover all that he would ever need to know,
          "So are you."

that sixty-second spark gave rise
to gales between their lips, their
speech, that storm, their breath
tore houses down, and cedars
bowed to them . . .
they lie exhausted now
in the woods for miles around.

●

Calvin looked to where her voice had pointed, up, and in those stars
he saw the twinkle in the eyes of advertising's ideal man
     and could not jettison the thought.
"You wouldn't have said that six months ago," he told her,
     and just then she believed him.
Deep in the hollow of her sum and substance, the trembling,
       it was either admit to this thing now
       or bleed until it wasn't true.

Weightless

So much can fall away so quickly —
mass, concerns, acres — it's funny sometimes
how even the ground you walk turns alien,
distant as the littered bottom of a lake
with all its rusted and forgotten hulks,
the felonies and accidents long gone.

Two thousand feet above it — living through the push
of a sixty-degree banking turn for the better,
twice the force of gravity, and still,
at this height, at this speed, weightless.

Defying that force at last, his guts gone weak,
a basket of kittens mewing for milk,
yet here was an eagle, bearing them back to the nest,
        unsure whether to eat
        or raise them.

Weightless and forgotten to himself,
this isn't Calvin, tanned and thin, not the grain
of what he is inside his mind, the one and only
form of himself he has come to believe:
        a small and bashful boy
        weighing five hundred pounds.

●

Don't look now, child. You're doing it, arms outstretched,
wind in your face, flying, soaring, looping the loop,
shooting the moon, buzzing your lips like a prop,
and far below the teeny dot of your shadow leaping
      over roadways and rooftops.

No time to think that landing might strip this gift, my child,
      or that every return to Earth
      is to waken in some unforgiving yard without your lunch.
      In time there may be much heavier yokes to bear,
but you're free of them for now. Every boy you've ever been can sense
      the flex of new beginnings.
But still you can hear, however faint, however faraway,
      somewhere, perhaps in your twenties,
          your thirties, somewhere . . .

the fat lady singing.

Acknowledgements

Some of these poems have appeared in *The Literary Review of Canada*, *Kiss Machine*, *Queen Street Quarterly*, *Taddle Creek*, *Descant*, *The Toronto Small Press Fair Instant Anthology*, or have been broadcast on CBC Radio One and CIUT Radio 89.5 FM. In many cases the poems first appeared in slightly different versions. The poem "Alone in the Bathroom He Removed His Shirt" originally appeared in *Burn* (ECW PRESS 2000).

The author wishes to thank the Ontario Arts Council for its generous financial support.

Thank you to Michael Holmes for his editorial vision and faith. Thanks also to Jack David, Amy Logan, Tania Craan, Mary Bowness, and everyone at ECW PRESS for working with me on this.

For those who have helped to bring this book into existence and/or those who helped me get through the writing of it, I give thanks: to my mother and father for everything; to Dennis Lee and Susan Perly for their guidance; to Lynn Crosbie for her encouragement; to A.F. Moritz for his kindness and knowledge; to David McGimpsey for knowing all too well; to Peter Darbyshire and Jonathan Bennett forever; to George Murray and Ailsa Craig for their courage; to Adam Levin for Wittgenstein, and fried dough; to Mike O'Connor for his trust; to Leon Rooke for Eden Mills; to Conan Tobias for *Taddle Creek*; to Patrick Woodcock for groceries and beer; to John Stiles for mystifying conversations with no beginning, middle, or end; to Carleton Wilson for his weasel genius; to Silas White for a hawk-eyed proofread; to Patrick Crean and Katja Pantzar for a great year; to Jana Prikryl for her patience; to Marcia Mack for Toronto Island; to wherever my next meal is coming from; and to my friend Ronan Quinn . . . for the lift.